101 Ways to Make Friends:

Ideas and conversation starters for people with disabilities and their supporters

Aaron Johannes and Susan Kurliak

Copyright by Aaron Johannes and Susan Kurliak

All rights reserved

ISBN 978-0-557-04213-5

*To Gary, Zev, Michael, Ben,
and our Spectrum family*

> *"I have an intuitive grasp on a possibility that inclusion can lead to transformation in social and economic relationships."*
>
> Judith Snow

Index

1. Say hello to the next person you see
2. Make eye contact; smile
3. Tell people you want to make friends
4. Make a list of everyone you know
5. Walk into anything an equal, with much to be proud of
6. Use affirmations
7. Make a community inventory
8. Find out what's special about your city or neighbourhood
9. Become a "regular"
10. Take part in a run for charity
11. Host a games night
12. Respect differences
13. Walk or take transit as much as you can
14. If you're shy or need help – find a leader for your own "friends" project
15. Still feeling shy? Start with something small
16. Decide to accept the next invitation that comes your way
17. Rehearse what you want to say ahead of time
18. Have an address book that works for you
19. Make a relationship journal about each of your friends
20. Dream a friend!
21. Support your local amateur sports teams
22. Notice other people who are alone
23. Have a yard sale but make the point of it getting to know others
24. Have a meeting with your supporters about your friends, and make a plan
25. Involve your family in the planning
26. Get to know your neighbours
27. Have an open house and invite the neighbours in
28. Read your community newspapers
29. Deliver the community newspaper
30. Join a church or synagogue, or find some other spiritual gathering place
31. Take advantage of the social opportunities at your place of worship
32. Be true to yourself
33. What are you good at? Teach a skill that you love
34. Go to the gym
35. Learn to say "hello" in different languages
36. Try a new look – see who says hello

37. Have one good joke you can tell
38. Take photos and show them around
39. Stay on top of some current events and look for opportunities to discuss them
40. Go to the local pub to watch the game instead of watching it at home alone
41. Family members can be friends too
42. Take a multi-cultural cooking class
43. Celebrate all the holidays
44. Put "friends and family" at the top of the agenda for planning meetings
45. Share what you love – lend someone a book or DVD you enjoyed
46. Make it a habit to be the one who always welcomes the new person
47. Take a class at the local community centre
48. Resolve conflicts peacefully and move on; don't hold a grudge
49. Take initiative; suggest something fun or interesting
50. Ask the agency that supports you to make personal support networks a priority
51. Step outside of your usual circle
52. Be the kind of friend you'd like to meet
53. Sit in a different spot and meet new people
54. Draw others to you (the law of attraction)
55. Build your family tree
56. Get a facebook account
57. Take a workshop on internet safety
58. Practise asking people for their phone number
59. Have friends' phone numbers and email addresses handy
60. Have a phone that works for you
61. Have a supply of personalized business cards
62. Connect with your past
63. Organize a "girls' night out" or a "boys' night out"
64. Send postcards to people when you go traveling
65. Compliment someone on something you've noticed about them
66. Get your staff to step back
67. Talk about pets
68. Organize a camping trip
69. Shop locally
70. Go to the movie everyone is talking about
71. Be a neighbourhood trick-or-treat stop at Hallowe'en
72. Communicate as clearly and confidently as you can
73. Be a good listener

74. Join a community choir
75. Collect something, and talk to others who share your passion
76. Show an interest in what others are saying
77. Notice what someone else is good at and ask them about it
78. Get a job
79. Be an advocate or sign up with an advocacy agency to mentor someone
80. Gather people who all want to expand their social lives or social skills
81. Learn to lead
82. Give yourself permission to miss the mark
83. Practise introducing yourself to new people
84. Stay hopeful
85. Pay attention to non-verbal cues
86. Notice people with great social skills
87. Invite people over for a holiday meal
88. Rake a neighbour's lawn, or shovel their snow
89. Recognize other people's accomplishments
90. Join a committee
91. Organize a fundraiser for the charity of your choice
92. Be the person who remembers birthdays
93. Join in the fun
94. Host a potluck picnic
95. Learn the art of small talk
96. So... You want to get romantic?
97. Set goals
98. Imagine a future with friends
99. See yourself as a community builder
100. Make the most of each new day
101.

Introduction

For more than twenty years, we have been involved in conversations with folks with disabilities and their supporters about relationships – feelings of loss, feelings of connection – "am I doing too much?" "am I not doing enough?" "is anyone else out there?" – fears and uncertainty that people with disabilities are not accepted as citizens in their communities. We've talked with parents of all ages who are planning for a future when their son or daughter will not have them to rely on (or refusing to plan because they can't bear to think about it) and with young people transitioning into a future in which they will be more independent and will need friends to rely on for practical and emotional reasons. But most of these talks have occurred "off the side of our desks" and within other planning contexts.

In 2007 we took on a demonstration project through Community Living British Columbia in which we examined the support networks (family, friends, advocates, co-workers, neighbours) of eight people with disabilities. Part of the project was to look at ways to expand the networks of those who had involved friends and family and, for half of the people involved, who had no one they could depend on in their lives, to look at ways in which people with few or no unpaid relationships could be assisted to develop a network of supporters.

What we discovered quite soon was that many of the things we assumed were in place for everyone our agency supported were not actually happening. Ouch. People didn't have address books, they didn't have trusted facilitators or family members helping them negotiate the often fraught field of relationships, nor was there a plan to fill that gap. Things happened, or had happened, and no one really debriefed or processed events with them and allowed them to go on, wiser and more (or less) open to the next relationship. Instead, grief and confusion accrued. So we got a chance to figure out some of those things. Our Executive Director, Ernie Baatz, was supportive of the project throughout and said, "This is some of the most important learning we've done in 20 years."

Around the province three other groups worked on similar projects and what all of us discovered is that a) the support of unpaid relationships is an idea in its infancy – we might be doing a great job of supporting people in their communities and expanding our ideas of what folks' lives can look like, but we're just beginning to delve into the idea of natural relationships that are supported by systems; b) that unpaid relationships can be fostered and strengthened with very simple ideas that are easily put into place and conversations that are easy (and fun) to have; and perhaps most importantly, c) it is POSSIBLE for folks with disabilities to be and have great friends and supporters, even if they are currently isolated.

Later, we expanded the conversation and tried to find others who were also interested in these ideas, to build a network of mutually supportive friends, one person at a time. We've found that the hardest thing for people to hold on to in all of this is hopefulness. We met families who were doing incredible things with their family member with a disability, but felt they weren't doing enough. Folks with disabilities who worked hard on their networks, had taken all the classes, done all the homework, and still felt inadequate. A number of things became evident:

- The most important thing is to stay hopeful.

- Find ways to give leadership for their relationships to the folks we support.

- Identify clear, reasonable goals.

- Make a place for the conversations that need to happen.

- Don't assume anything.

So, on the one hand, where networks are happening in a conscious way, people are not feeling successful because they have rarely identified what success is and, instead, are thinking "we could be doing more." On the other hand, where it's not happening, people don't know how to proceed. So we started keeping this list of "things that are missing and easy to fix." An address book, for example. Life with an address book that works for you is completely different from life without an address book. One has ready, simple, self-directed access to connections - pick up your address book, find a friend, make a date to do something, build the relationship. Those moments - movies, going for coffee, an impromptu bowling afternoon or a walk through a park - are the building blocks that create the relationship that we depend on when we're ill or in distress or facing a decision that we're unsure about. No address book = no bowling date = no one to call when you're off to emergency or when you get bad news and the professional says "Is there someone I should call?" Likewise, setting a concrete goal: "In the next three months I will take a cooking class and invite a fellow student to come to my house to practise a recipe." You can either succeed or you can be working on it, learning more about how to proceed to success but once you've got the goal you've got hope and, if you reach it, something to celebrate and build on. "I want friends" or "We want him to have friends" is a much harder thing to pin down and be successful with.

Different people, with and without disabilities, have different address books - some are written, some are on their computers, some are in the memories of their phones - but they have those numbers and can use them. We kept meeting folks with disabilities who had no address books. We'd talk to their staff teams and hear "well, they lost it," as if that explained why it didn't exist. We went back to the people who had address books and asked them if they ever lost them, and, heck, it turned out that we've all lost address books of various kinds and it doesn't mean we can yet do without one; what it means is that we need an "address book backup plan" – keeping everything on the computer and reprinting it, or having a second address book with important contacts written down in case the first one gets lost. We made an initial list of indicators of relationships, and "has an address book," was one of the items on the list. We predicted 80% of the folks would have address books, which was the reverse of what we found (80% did not).

This is an early stage in our research and experiences of this aspect of community living and we're looking forward to seeing and doing more and talking to more folks and their supporters; we've already begun to seize opportunities to travel and meet people and talk to them about their successes and challenges in this area. But, already, it has become apparent to us that these are conversations that many, many, many people need to have in all kinds of situations – individuals, communities, organizations where people gather, children, schools. And no one is more experienced or able to show us the way than the people who are at the heart of this discussion, those who fought to close institutions and overcome age-old stereotypes to gain the right of citizenship. We often talk about how systems, not just structures, can become institutional – and how the language of community living continues to separate people by emphasizing differences instead of similarities (even referring to it as "community living" implies an alternative – institutional living – which remains a very real threat to people in other provinces and other parts of the world where institutions continue to thrive). The service system that has evolved over the past couple of decades has allowed people to be physically integrated, but many remain socially isolated, surrounded by paid staff and professionals in special classrooms or programs for groups of adults with disabilities. Funding and eligibility criteria drive the planning, not relationships. The very systems that were designed to include people continue to separate them from community; not having friends increases their risk of isolation.

Some of the best ideas in this book came from folks with disabilities who have built their own personal support networks, often without (or even despite) our assistance as paid supporters. The lessons to be learned from their example cannot be understated. The idea that people with developmental disabilities can not only live in community, but have valued and reciprocal relationships as friends and neighbours, represents a huge shift in thinking. As service providers, we must learn to facilitate, rather than supplant, these natural relationships – to expand our thinking about the gifts and contributions folks have to offer and be appreciated for.

The more we look at this issue of personal support networks, the more clear – and impassioned – we become about our mission as an agency. We're not just providing services...we're building community.

We hope that the work of so many people who have brought us to this pivotal point in our history means that institutions will never re-open and that large and "institutionalised" support systems will continue to downsize and personalise and that "community living" will not signify the threat of the alternative but will come to demonstrate the capacity for leadership that is in our field.

Susan Kurliak and Aaron Johannes
Spectrum Society for Community Living (2009)

101 Ways to Make Friends:

Ideas and conversation starters for people with disabilities and their supporters

1. Say hello to the next person you see

2. Make eye contact; smile

Notice who smiles back

3. Tell people you want to make friends

It's like finding a new job – the more people who know, the more likely the connections you could make

4. Make a list of everyone you know

Call and invite one person out

5. Walk into anything an equal, with much to be proud of

If you don't know what it is about you that people love, ask them

6. Use affirmations

We can replace the negative thoughts that pop into our minds, like "no-one wants to go to the movies with me," with happy thoughts, like "I'm a good friend" – these are called affirmations.

Write some down and put them where you'll see them often

7. Make a community inventory

Map your neighbourhood and the opportunities that are there

8. Find out what's special about your city or neighbourhood

...a certain festival or group? They're looking for you to help out – sell programs, walk on stilts, serve tea

9. Become a "regular"

Take the paper to the coffee shop every Saturday instead of reading it at home

10. Take part in a run for charity

If you don't run, volunteer to hand out water, or take part in some other way

11. Host a games night

12. Respect differences

Enjoy diversity

13. Walk or take transit as much as you can

The same neighbours are out walking at the same time…the same people are on the same buses.

Nobody ever made a friend driving alone or being driven by staff

14. If you're shy or need help – find a leader for your own "friends" project

People often want a way to help. How will you empower them?

15. Still feeling shy? Start with something small

Sometimes people believe they are shy in social situations, but what they mean is that walking into a room where anything could happen is *too much* – they might need a smaller focus, like helping to serve drinks, or greeting people at the door.

Every journey begins with a single step

16. Decide to accept the next invitation that comes your way

...no matter what it is! Be open to (just about) anything

17. Rehearse what you want to say ahead of time

Afterwards, think about how it went and what you might do differently next time

18. Have an address book that works for you

Whatever form it takes, carry it with you and write down new people as you meet them

19. Make a relationship journal about each of your friends

Write down how you know them, what you usually do together, their contact information, updates – then put them all together in a binder called "My Network" and make it part of the orientation for new staff who come to support you

20. Dream a friend!

What kind of friend would you like to have? What do you imagine you would do together?

21. Support your local amateur sports teams

Find out the schedule for the soccer or softball league in your area and pick a team to support – or take in a hockey game at the local arena.

Keep showing up and you'll get to know the other spectators

22. Notice other people who are alone

We might think we're the loneliest person in the room, but we're usually wrong.

Take responsibility for introducing yourself and asking people to join you – later on they might tell you how much it meant to them

23. Have a yard sale but make the point of it getting to know others

Serve lemonade, have name tags – don't worry if you don't sell anything

24. Have a meeting with your supporters about your friends, and make a plan

25. Involve your family in the planning

Often they have long memories of who you knew and what you said in the past, and great ideas – and are looking for ways to be helpful. Some of the best leaders are grandparents and children

26. Get to know your neighbours

27. Have an open house and invite the neighbours in

Get known for your barbecued turkey or lasagne…

…or for being brave enough to host an open house

28. Read your community newspapers

They're full of things to do, coupons, contests, potential connections and articles about people you might meet

29. Deliver the community newspaper

Take on a small route that will give you time to chat

30. Join a church or synagogue, or find some other spiritual gathering place

31. Take advantage of the social opportunities at your place of worship

Stay for coffee hour...

...introduce yourself to the person in charge.

Ask how you can be a more involved member of the congregation or group

32. Be true to yourself

Be proud of who you are and
show people you can stand up for
what you believe in.

Don't compromise yourself or
your beliefs just to be accepted.

Being a friend
is the
opposite of
being a bully

33. What are you good at? Teach a skill that you love

34. Go to the gym

Do the same thing, at the same place, at the same time, every week

35. Learn to say "hello" in different languages

Start with one or two languages – to say "hello" to everyone on earth, you'd need to learn almost 3,000 languages.

If that seems hard, just wave!

36. Try a new look – see who says hello

37. Have one good joke you can tell

Practise it so you're ready when there's an uncomfortable gap in the conversation – be known as the person who made everyone feel comfortable

38. Take photos and show them around

Make albums, frame your pictures, upload them to online sites – share your visions

39. Stay on top of some current events and look for opportunities to discuss them

Whether it's politics that interests you, or entertainment news, you can connect with people by discussing what you've read in the paper or seen on t.v.

40. Go to the local pub to watch the game instead of watching it at home alone

Be part of cheering on your team

41. Family members can be friends too

Think about the people in your extended family – siblings, cousins, aunts, uncles, nieces, nephews, grandparents...

Who might you get to know better? What other family relationships might you explore?

42. Take a multi-cultural cooking class

Make new things and share meals

43. Celebrate all the holidays

Wear green on St. Patrick's Day and meet Irish people;

give out heart-shaped cookies for Valentine's; be the spirit of Christmas present...

...make everything you do be about potential connections

44. Put "friends and family" at the top of the agenda for planning meetings

Spend some time talking about it before everyone gets tired of talking

45. Share what you love – lend someone a book or DVD you enjoyed

46. Make it a habit to be the one who always welcomes the new person

They'll never forget how you made them feel welcome

47. Take a class at the local community centre

48. Resolve conflicts peacefully and move on; don't hold a grudge

We're here to make friends, not enemies.

When people wish "we could all just get along," aspire to be the one they'll think of as a role model

49. Take initiative; suggest something fun or interesting

Be the one to make the first move

50. Ask the agency that supports you to make personal support networks a priority

Staff will be more likely to feel they have permission to focus on developing relationships if it's part of everything from job descriptions to evaluations to program monitoring

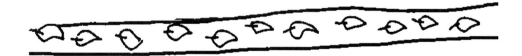

51. Step outside of your usual circle

Spend time with children, or elderly people, or people from other cultures

52. Be the kind of friend you'd like to meet

Demonstrate a positive attitude

Always seek solutions (don't complain)

Avoid gossip

53. Sit in a different spot and meet new people

If you always do what you've always done, you'll always get what you've always got

54. Draw others to you (the law of attraction)

Build your own interests so that people have something to ask you about

55. Build your family tree

Do some research and see
who else is out there,
waiting for you to call...

56. Get a facebook account

...or join some other social networking site

Everything about facebook is designed to connect you (or re-connect you) with others

57. Take a workshop on internet safety

Learn how to safely share your information online.

Suggest to the teacher that the class share email addresses and see if anyone wants to keep in touch

58. Practise asking people for their phone number

Asking people for their phone number is a great social cue – you're letting them know you're interested.

You'll want to practise; most of us do not know how to ask for a phone number

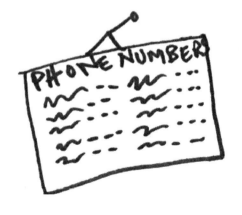

59. Have friends' phone numbers and email addresses handy

Keep them in sight so you are reminded to stay in contact

60. Have a phone that works for you

61. Have a supply of personalized business cards

Make some up on the computer and print them out in small batches – give them to people you'd like to see again.

Or make fridge magnets with your phone number

62. Connect with your past

Who do you remember... where are they now?

63. Organize a "girls' night out" or a "boys' night out"

Something in common, simply stated ("we're all girls") can lead to closer connections ("we're all girls who like karaoke – let's get together every month")

64. Send postcards to people when you go traveling

By the time you get home, they're eager to talk about what you saw

65. Compliment someone on something you've noticed about them

66. Get your staff to step back

...so others can step in.

Place your own order at the coffee shop. Accept help from another customer instead of having your staff do everything.

Fading support is one of the most important skills for staff to learn

67. Talk about pets

If you don't have any pets, ask people about theirs – it's simple and not too personal and it can lead to other conversations

68. Organize a camping trip

There's nothing like shared holiday memories of sticky s'mores in the rain to cement a relationship

69. Shop locally

Get to know the stores in your neighbourhood or go to the farmer's market

70. Go to the movie everyone is talking about

...then talk about it

People love talking about movies

71. Be a neighbourhood trick-or-treat stop at Hallowe'en

Go all out –

carve pumpkins, put up decorations…

…and of course, have great treats to give out!

72. Communicate as clearly and confidently as you can

If you have an augmentative communication system, include important names, places and events so you can talk about the things that matter to you

73. Be a good listener

74. Join a community choir

Do you like to sing?

Look into community or church choirs in your area – they are often looking for new members

75. Collect something, and talk to others who share your passion

...coins, hats, ceramic elephants, Elvis memorabilia...

76. Show an interest in what others are saying

Don't dominate the conversation

77. Notice what someone else is good at and ask them about it

Letting someone know you notice their strengths is never a mistake

78. Get a job

...there is something useful for everyone to do.

Most people find their friends at school or work

79. Be an advocate or sign up with an advocacy agency to mentor someone

Sometimes it is easier to make sure someone else is heard than to speak up for yourself. But one thing leads to another...

80. Gather people who all want to expand their social lives or social skills

81. Learn to lead

The most powerful and dedicated personal support networks are the ones that are "managed" by the person with a disability – the degree of disability doesn't seem to matter if they have the right supports.

How can the person you support lead their network?

82. Give yourself permission to miss the mark

Nothing is going to be perfect the first time – to make one friend we need to meet a whole lot of people who won't be our friends

Just keep trying

83. Practise introducing yourself to new people

Nobody is born knowing these skills

84. Stay hopeful

*"Where there is misery
Bring expectancy
And surely we can change
Surely we can change
Something"*

...David Crowder,

"Surely We Can Change"

(Listen to music that inspires you)

85. Pay attention to non-verbal cues

Think about the messages you're sending through your facial expressions and body posture.

How might you look more friendly and open?

86. Notice people with great social skills

Who do you know who has lots of friends and seems comfortable in any situation?

Learn from them

87. Invite people over for a holiday meal

Host Christmas dinner at your place this year – or find a community meal for Thanksgiving and start a new tradition

"Invite a Neighbour for Dinner" day is the second Saturday in January

88. Rake a neighbour's lawn, or shovel their snow

89. Recognize other people's accomplishments

Always be ready to congratulate them

90. Join a committee

Organizations are always looking for people to sit on committees.

Volunteer for the social committee and help organize an event that brings people together

91. Organize a fundraiser for the charity of your choice

Pick something fun like a bake sale, and invite others to help – maybe Mrs. Smith from next door will donate a loaf of her famous banana bread...

92. Be the person who remembers birthdays

93. Join in the fun

Don't wait for an invitation

94. Host a potluck picnic

Cook for friends

95. Learn the art of small talk

"How are you?"

"What do you think of this weather?"

Think of a few phrases to get past the initial "hello"

96. So... You want to get romantic?

Having a boyfriend or girlfriend involves a whole other set of skills that nobody is born knowing...

...but it might be the most important thing to you.

Talk to people you know and trust – find out how other singles in your area meet people

97. Set goals

Be realistic, and hopeful too. Write down your goals (the chance of success greatly increases)

If all you want is a quiet companion to take long hikes with, and you find one, your goal is accomplished…

…nobody else can say how many friends you need, or what your relationships *should* look like

98. Imagine a future with friends

Where will you be in 5 years? 10 years? Who will be your friends then?

99. See yourself as a community builder

On a micro-level everyone wants someone who cares about them. On a macro-level by caring about this, we're caring about something greater than any one of us, which is the community that we are all part of. It's big stuff and folks with disabilities and their supporters know more about community than almost anyone. Stronger communities have more resilience, are safer, healthier, have more capacity, can deal with difficulty, are more fun to be part of, are more compassionate. They are not sad, hopeless, exhausted or downtrodden. All over the world people are trying to create community.

YOU are a leader, a vital part of something big and important and you got here by walking through fire...through a history of institutions and disenfranchisement. No one knows more about leading the world in regaining quality of life than YOU.

100. Make the most of each new day

*Yesterday is history
tomorrow is a mystery
today is a gift –
that's why it's called "the present"*

101.

What might you do?

101 Ways to Make Friends:

Ideas and Conversation Starters for People with Disabilities and Their Supporters

is a project of Spectrum Society for Community Living

www.spectrumsociety.org
www.101friends.ca

or find us on facebook, search on "Spectrum"

The ideas in this book are based on many conversations with folks with disabilities, individually and as part of groups like People First, their friends, families and teams that have all shared with us their expertise, dreams and goals and in the process have made us part of their networks, for which we are grateful.

Everyone has great stories about how they made friends. Maybe you've done something that others could learn from – we'd love to hear from you!

Email us at psn@spectrumsociety.org

About the authors

Susan Kurliak
Director, Communications and Quality Assurance
Spectrum Society for Community Living

Susan has worked in community living for nearly 30 years. She coordinated recreation programs and volunteer services for the Autism Society of B.C. while attending university, and worked for a number of local community agencies prior to co-founding Spectrum Society in 1987. As a Co-Director of Spectrum, Susan oversees the information management and infrastructure that supports Spectrum's services to individuals and families in the greater Vancouver area. She lives in Burnaby with her two sons.

Aaron Johannes
Director, Community Based Services
Spectrum Society for Community Living

Aaron is a Co-Director of Spectrum and a proud family member to people with disabilities. He and his partner have been foster-parents for ten years to teens with significant challenges and also have a young son; among various other roles he has been gratified to learn from, he has been a provincial advisor for People First, a facilitator with the Vela Microboard Association and a writer. His passions are art, literature, business philosophy and gardening. *"My drawings in this book will remind many of P.A.T.H.s, which stands for 'Planning Alternative Tomorrows with Hope' graphic note-taking was developed by Inclusion Press (Jack Pearpoint, Marsha Forest, John O'Brien) - it's a process I love."*

We'd like to thank so many people for their sharing, help and support while we worked on this book but particularly the folks and families who spoke with us, our leadership team at Spectrum Society, Community Living B.C., the other agencies involved in the demonstration projects that inspired this book, and Michael Walsh of Kaizen Consulting who encouraged us and helped us create the space where this was possible.

Aaron and Susan regularly conduct workshops on this and many other topics around North America.

Feedback from recent participants:

"Thank you for an excellent workshop. It will help us on our uncharted journey to support my son"

"Presented in an easy to understand format (with simple language)"

"Great day, thank you!"

"[You] spread hopefulness in the universe; the question isn't whether the glass is half empty or half full, it is 'how do we fill up the glass?'"

"The overwhelmingly positive evaluations are a testament to your hard work. Thank you so much"

For more information, contact psn@spectrumsociety.org or visit us at www.101friends.ca

LaVergne, TN USA
22 February 2011
217389LV00006B/1-80/P